# Porcupines

by Emily Green

BELLWETHER MEDIA · MINNEAPOLIS, MN

Note to Librarians, Teachers, and Parents:

**Blastoff! Readers** are carefully developed by literacy experts and combine standards-based content with developmentally appropriate text.

**Level 1** provides the most support through repetition of high-frequency words, light text, predictable sentence patterns, and strong visual support.

**Level 2** offers early readers a bit more challenge through varied simple sentences, increased text load, and less repetition of high-frequency words.

**Level 3** advances early-fluent readers toward fluency through increased text and concept load, less reliance on visuals, longer sentences, and more literary language.

**Level 4** builds reading stamina by providing more text per page, increased use of punctuation, greater variation in sentence patterns, and increasingly challenging vocabulary.

**Level 5** encourages children to move from "learning to read" to "reading to learn" by providing even more text, varied writing styles, and less familiar topics.

Whichever book is right for your reader, Blastoff! Readers are the perfect books to build confidence and encourage a love of reading that will last a lifetime!

This edition first published in 2011 by Bellwether Media, Inc.

No part of this publication may be reproduced in whole or in part without written permission of the publisher. For information regarding permission, write to Bellwether Media, Inc., Attention: Permissions Department, 5357 Penn Avenue South, Minneapolis, MN 55419.

Library of Congress Cataloging-in-Publication Data
Green, Emily K., 1966-
Porcupines / by Emily Green.
   p. cm. – (Backyard wildlife)
Includes bibliographical references and index.
Summary: "Developed by literacy experts for students in kindergarten through grade three, this book introduces porcupines to young readers through leveled text and related photos"–Provided by publisher.
ISBN 978-1-60014-562-9 (hardcover : alk. paper)
 1. Porcupines–Juvenile literature.  I. Title.
QL737.R652G743 2011
599.35'97–dc22                              2010034533

Text copyright © 2011 by Bellwether Media, Inc. BLASTOFF! READERS and associated logos are trademarks and/or registered trademarks of Bellwether Media, Inc.

Printed in the United States of America, North Mankato, MN.

010111      1176

# Contents

Porcupines are **rodents**. They live in forests, grasslands, and deserts.

Some porcupines
climb trees
to find food.
Sharp **claws** help
porcupines climb.

claws

Porcupines eat bark, plants, nuts, and fruits.

Porcupines have four long front teeth. They use them to **gnaw** on food.

Porcupines have soft fur that keeps them warm. They have thick **guard hairs** that keep them dry.

Porcupines also have stiff hairs called **quills**. Quills have sharp, pointed tips.

Quills usually lie flat. Porcupines raise their quills if they **sense** danger.

Porcupines stamp their feet and hiss when they see **predators**. They shake their tails to loosen their quills.

Porcupines use their quills to poke predators that get too close. Ouch!

# Glossary

**claws**—sharp, curved nails on the feet of porcupines; claws help porcupines climb.

**gnaw**—to bite or nibble on something for a long time

**guard hairs**—thick hairs that are longer than an animal's fur; guard hairs help keep an animal dry.

**predators**—animals that hunt other animals for food

**quills**—stiff hairs with sharp, pointed tips; porcupines use their quills to poke predators that get too close.

**rodents**—a group of small animals that usually gnaw on their food

**sense**—to become aware of

# To Learn More

## AT THE LIBRARY

Lang, Aubrey. *Baby Porcupines*. Toronto, Ont.:
Fitzhenry and Whiteside, 2005.

Lester, Helen. *A Porcupine Named Fluffy*.
Boston, Mass.: Houghton Mifflin, 1986.

Macken, JoAnn Early. *Porcupines*. Milwaukee,
Wisc.: Weekly Reader Early Learning, 2005.

## ON THE WEB

Learning more about
porcupines is as easy as 1, 2, 3.

1. Go to www.factsurfer.com.

2. Enter "porcupines" into the search box.

3. Click the "Surf" button and you will see a
   list of related Web sites.

With factsurfer.com, finding more information
is just a click away.

# Index

The images in this book are reproduced through the courtesy of: Tony Rix, front cover, p. 11; AlaskaStock/Photolibrary, p. 5; Juan Martinez, pp. 5 (left), 9 (left, right); Mares Lucian, p. 5 (middle); Kushch Dmitry, p. 5 (right); Jack Milchanowshi/Photolibrary, p. 7; Joe Austin Photography/Alamy, p. 9; Mauro Rodrigues, p. 9 (middle); S Muller/Photolibrary, pp. 13, 19; Ultrashock, p. 14; Wayne Lynch/Photolibrary, p. 15; James Hager/Photolibrary, p. 17; Anke van Wyk, p. 20; Thomas Kitchin & Victoria Hurst/Alamy, p. 21.